Learn by Handwriting

Practice Workbook

Cursive 3

The Lord's Prayer

Christian Prayers

memorescribe.com

The Lord's Prayer - Christian Prayers - Cursive 3
Memorescribe Learn by Handwriting Practice Workbook
Copyright © 2024 by Globaloft, LLC
Alpharetta, GA

Publishing Credits | Authors, Editors, Interior & Cover Designers: Jessica Cobo and Victor Cobo

Memorescribe Product # PNCC3PE

TABLE OF CONTENTS

Dearest Persevering Writer,

   One of my proudest achievements at the age of 8 was learning to read and write in cursive. Learning cursive whisked me away on adventures as I read my grandparents' beautiful handwritten travel postcards. Even today, I cherish my grandmother's handwritten recipe card as well as her personalized book inscriptions that I have the chance to re-read as I pass those books along to my children.

   Many of us can remember the time before handwriting was eclipsed by digital communication. Consider the present reality, all the text messages and emails we read but barely remember and rarely keep as a treasured memory. While there are innumerable benefits to computer use and digital communication, handwriting remains a powerful, valuable skill.

   Memorescribe Learn by Handwriting workbooks began as a passion project. When working to help my child develop handwriting skills, I discovered an opportunity to use handwriting practice time to learn and reinforce important educational information. Memorescribe workbooks offer you the opportunity to practice and develop your personal, unique handwriting style while taking advantage of the time to learn something new or reinforce information you learned in the past.

   Wherever you are on your journey, no matter your age or handwriting ability, my hope is that Memorescribe's Learn by Handwriting workbooks will send you off on your own learning adventures, travelling as far as your handwriting will take you.

                                        Jessica

Memorescribe Learn by Handwriting workbooks create a fun and meaningful opportunity to commit educational information to memory while you practice your handwriting because we believe handwriting is an invaluable skill. **Learn as you write with Memorescribe!**

IMPORTANCE OF HANDWRITING

1. Writing by hand is a **foundational educational skill** connected to academic progress and success.

2. Writing by hand **activates** different parts of **the brain** and can **boost** your **brain function**.

3. Writing by hand helps to **develop** the **small movements** and **coordination skills** needed **for success** in everyday life.

4. Handwriting notes helps to **organize thoughts** and **process information** more **deeply** which can lead to **better learning**, understanding, **retaining**, and recalling **information**.

5. A unique form of personal expression, handwriting can **display individual personality**, creative tendencies, and artistic craftsmanship as well as **verify identity**.

6. Writing by hand can help to **process emotions**, **set goals**, soothe and calm while encouraging **personal reflection** on experiences and circumstances.

7. Handwritten notes and documents convey a **memorable**, meaningful, **personal touch** and **demonstrate care** and thoughtfulness towards the recipient.

8. Preserving methods and styles of handwriting allows people groups and cultures the opportunity to **maintain heritage** and **safeguard history**.

Print and Cursive Handwriting

Print Handwriting, also known as Manuscript, is patterned after the style of letters commonly used in printed materials such as books, newspapers, or magazines. Each letter is written independently and is not connected to any other letter. To create print style handwriting, the writer lifts the pen or pencil from the paper after forming each letter. Print handwriting is simple and can often be easier to read than cursive style writing.

Cursive Handwriting is also known as Script, longhand, or joined-up writing. The scripted style of writing is created using connected, flowing letters which allows for faster, more elegant writing than print. Writers of cursive use single strokes to create letters without lifting the pen or pencil from the paper and connect the letters within the same word. Cursive handwriting is more intricate than print and can add a touch of sophistication whenever used.

With Memorescribe, *you can choose your handwriting style and text size.* For handwriting style, choose between print and cursive. For handwriting text size, choose from level 1, level 2, or level 3 in your selected style.

Workbooks are available in the following style and size options:

Books available in English, Spanish, and other languages.

Pencil Grip Tip:

Pinch the pencil between your thumb and first finger. Rest the pinched fingers with pencil on the middle finger. Curl the last two fingers into the palm of your hand for support as you rest your hand on the writing surface.

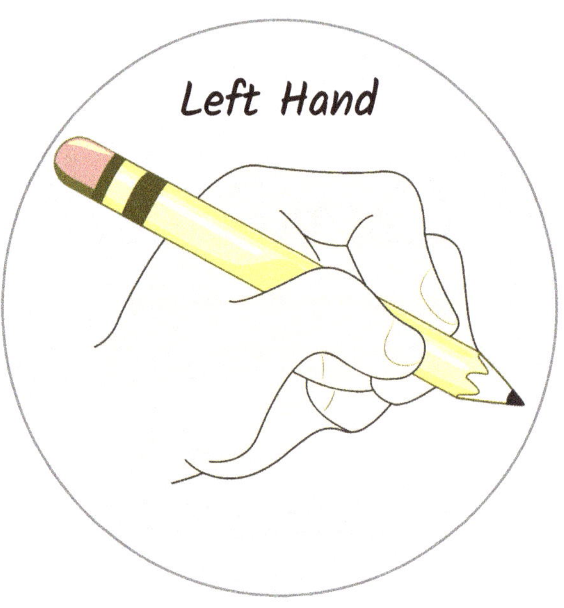

Supportive Handwriting Pencil Grip

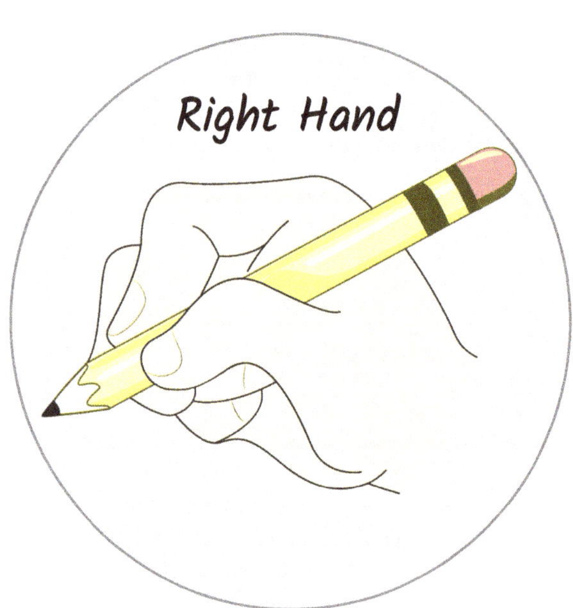

PRACTICE MAKES THE MASTER

The Lord's Prayer

Our Father who art in heaven,
hallowed be thy name.
Thy kingdom come. Thy will be done
on earth, as it is in heaven.
Give us this day our daily bread,
and forgive us our trespasses,
as we forgive those
who trespass against us,
and lead us not into temptation,
but deliver us from evil. Amen.

Our Father who art in heaven,

Our Father who art in heaven,

Our Father who art in heaven,

hallowed be thy name. Thy kingdom come.

hallowed be thy name. Thy kingdom come.

Thy will be done on earth, as it is in heaven.

Thy will be done on earth, as it is in heaven.

Give us this day our daily bread,

Give us this day our daily bread,

and forgive us our trespasses,

and forgive us our trespasses,

as we forgive those who trespass against us,

as we forgive those who trespass against us,

and lead us not into temptation,

and lead us not into temptation,

but deliver us from evil. Amen.

but deliver us from evil. Amen.

Directions:

Search to find the list of words hidden inside the puzzle. Words can go in any direction and can share letters.

```
P Q P V Y E X J I H Y J E X
P K F S A Z Z M E A D E L H
Z S G D P P T A O O J M O W
Z D F G R X V D F D D Q R K
V R D A R E T Y A S G B D V
B X Y E N F Q H T E W N P Q
D E W O L L A H H S R F I H
R A I E A I T E E S A B R K
H T R A E U V M R A H Y A P
Y E W G H I B E G P A Z M E
N L X K G H P Y R S N V S P
I X N R D J V K L E I N L O
H S O S W Q M N I R M Y B M
E F U T E M P T A T I O N V
```

BREAD	DELIVER	EARTH	FATHER
FORGIVE	HALLOWED	HEAVEN	KINGDOM
LORD	PRAYER	TEMPTATION	TRESPASSES

Directions: Use the clues below to discover the missing words. Words share letters where they cross in the puzzle.

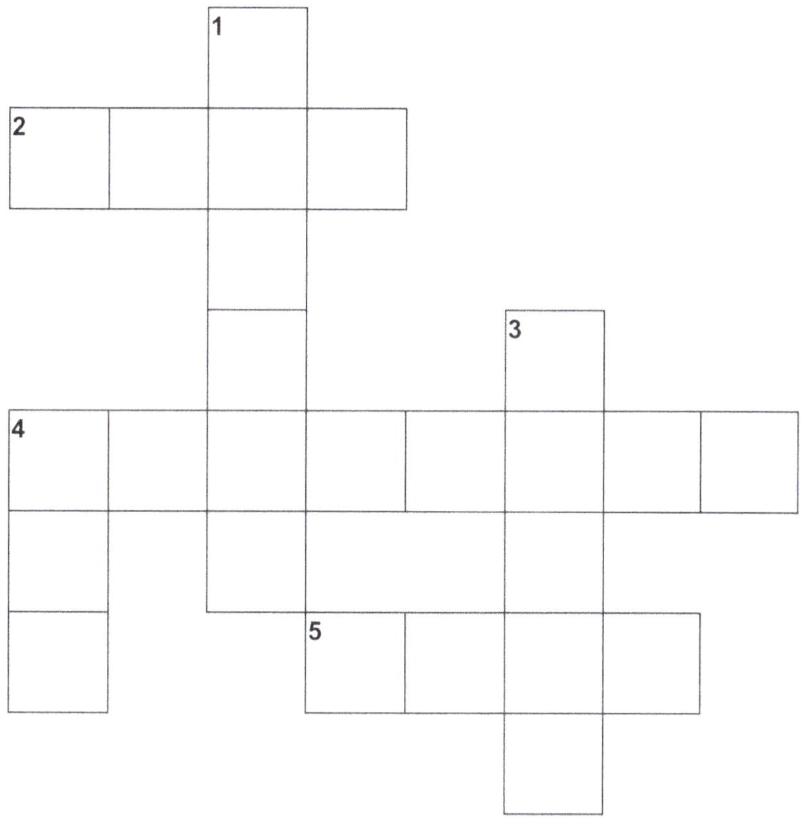

ACROSS

2. This means "it is true" or "let it be so"...

4. ...forgive those who _________________ against us...

5. ...thy _________________ be done...

DOWN

1. ...on earth as it is in _________________...

3. ...give us this day our _________________ bread...

4. ...hallowed be _________________ name...

Directions:

Search to find the list of words hidden inside the puzzle. Words can go in any direction and can share letters.

```
D  X  U  E  N  J  T  B  Z  D  D  H  E  S
C  Q  K  E  P  I  D  H  C  R  Q  A  S  T
A  U  S  Z  W  R  E  M  H  X  O  E  H  C
L  D  G  T  E  M  Y  C  T  B  N  A  W  O
T  P  O  Q  R  N  M  B  H  E  N  N  E  N
R  P  A  R  B  E  O  D  V  K  A  O  H  F
U  D  D  N  A  S  N  I  S  X  U  R  T  E
S  U  W  I  R  T  G  G  T  L  S  Y  T  S
T  T  Q  C  H  R  I  S  T  I  A  N  A  S
O  V  M  J  O  V  U  O  E  H  T  P  M  I
B  H  Z  F  I  I  B  E  N  J  A  E  K  O
L  S  H  N  T  I  M  X  Z  X  N  P  P  N
J  O  G  P  R  O  T  E  C  T  I  O  N  K
N  O  I  T  A  C  I  L  P  P  U  S  S  L
```

ADORATION	FORGIVENESS	PETITION	SUPPLICATION
CHRISTIAN	LUKE	MATTHEW	PROTECTION
THANKSGIVING	CONFESSION	STRENGTH	TRUST

Break Activity 4
Crossword

Directions: Use the clues below to discover the missing words. Words share letters where they cross in the puzzle.

ACROSS

3. Something bad that can do harm or cause hurt...

5. To set free or liberate...

6. Something that tempts, entices, or allures...

7. To take away the penalty for doing wrong...

DOWN

1. The place where the ruler is a king or queen...

2. The loving name Jesus uses to refer to God...

4. Something that is sacred or holy, worthy of praise...

Break Activities Solutions

Break Activity 1: **Word Search**

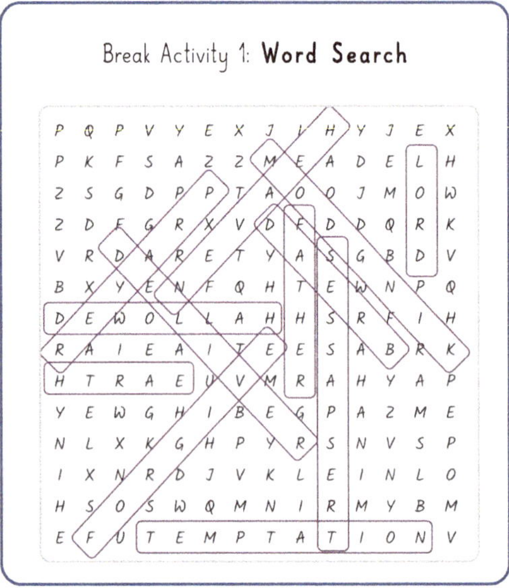

Break Activity 3: **Word Search**

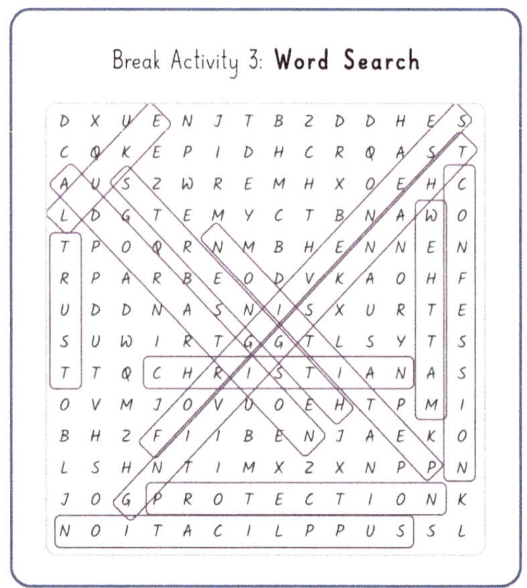

Break Activity 2: **Crossword**

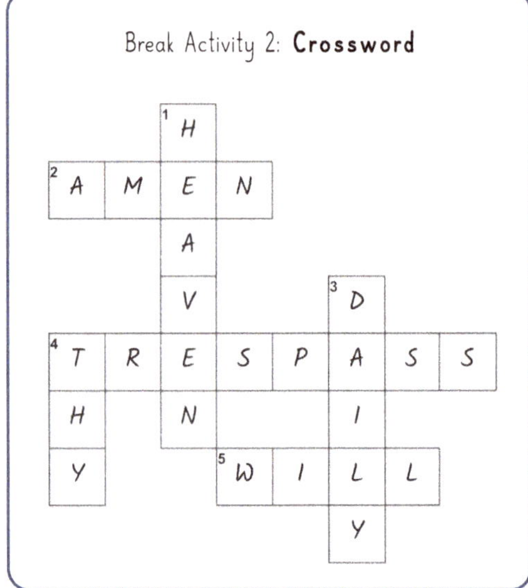

Break Activity 4: **Crossword**

Memorescribe Workbook Themes

Family

Nature

Math

Manners

Faith

Science

World

Sports

General Knowledge

and more to come!

Contact us for customized content for your organization or project.